P9-DCN-625

It's Not Easy Being Green
And Other Things to Consider

HYPERION
New York

It's Not Easy
Being Green

And Other Things to Consider

Jim Henson,
The Muppets,
and Friends

With drawings by Jim Henson
Edited by Cheryl Henson

All permissions to reproduce illustrations and quotes
appear on pages 187–192.

Copyright © 2005 The Jim Henson Company, Inc.

All rights reserved. No part of this book may be used or reproduced in
any manner whatsoever without the written permission of the Publisher.
Printed in the United States of America. For information address
Hyperion, 77 West 66th Street, New York, New York 10023-6298.

Library of Congress Cataloging-in-Publication Data
Henson, Jim.
It's not easy being green : and other things to consider / Jim Henson,
the Muppets, and friends ; with illustrations by Jim Henson ;
edited by Cheryl Henson.—1st ed.
p.   cm.
ISBN 1-4013-0242-4
1. Henson, Jim—Quotations. 2. Quotations, American.
I. Henson, Cheryl. II. Title.

PN1982.H46A25 2005
791.5'3'092—dc22   2005046334

Hyperion books are available for special promotions and premiums.
For details contact Michael Rentas, Assistant Director, Inventory
Operations, Hyperion, 77 West 66th Street, 11th floor,
New York, New York 10023, or call 212-456-0133.

Book design by Laurent Linn

FIRST EDITION

3 5 7 9 10 8 6 4 2

For John and Heather

Contents

Introduction BY CHERYL HENSON   1

Listen to Your Heart   9

Dynamite Determination   49

Together We'll Nab It   71

It Starts When We're Kids   101

A Part of Everything and Everyone   135

Contributors   173

Sources   187

Acknowledgments   193

Introduction

The song that my dad is best known for performing is "It's Not Easy Bein' Green," written by his long-term collaborator, Joe Raposo. We chose to use it as the title of this book because its lyrics capture not only the feelings of Kermit the Frog but a universal message that resonates with people the world over, a message that it's okay to be different, to embrace what makes you special, and to be proud of it.

Jim Henson's personality was very much like Kermit's, and in some ways this song echoes his own life and work. The choices that he made were unusual. He created his own path and walked it with confidence. He enjoyed life, he looked for a playful approach to everything that he did, and he found success and plenty to be grateful for along the way. For me it is the resolution of the song that fits him best: *"Green is cool and friendly like . . . and I think it's what I want to be."*

What you will find in these pages is a collection of quotes, many of them from my dad's characters and creative partners. We felt that this was the best approach because the world knew my father through the Muppet characters that he performed and the words of the writers with whom he worked. But this book also contains a lot of quotes from Jim himself that have been taken from interviews, personal notebooks, letters, and other writings, some being published now for the first time. Many of my favorites come from a six-month period in 1986 when I was working closely with him. During this time, we traveled extensively, including one trip that took us all the way around the world. Working in different countries and interacting with other cultures was fascinating to him and gave him much to consider.

My father was a thoughtful person. He was intrigued with the concept of the mind, how the brain works and where memories are stored. For him, the head was linked to the heart, and it was his heart that fueled everything he did. When my father got started on a project, he would look for inspiration from within. I remember when we were growing up, how he loved to take a chair out into the garden and sit quietly, away from the hustle and bustle of the home, and just be. There were five children, eight cats, two dogs, six rabbits, and a ferret in the household, so he needed to find quiet time to hear himself.

I believe that he always followed his heart and tried to focus on the things that truly mattered to him—joy, laughter, understanding, and a deeper sense of connectedness. That is why we titled the first chapter "Listen to Your Heart."

The second chapter is "Dynamite Determination." Although my father's inspiration came from the heart, he was a man who worked tirelessly and eagerly embraced opportunities to realize his dreams. Many people don't know that he did not set out to be a puppeteer. He grew up in rural Mississippi, and his first love was television and what he saw as its extraordinary potential to reach out to people. When he was seventeen years old, he went into the local TV station in Washington, D.C., near where his family was then living, and asked for a job. They didn't hire him, but he saw a sign on a bulletin board at the station looking for a puppeteer. He went to the local library, took out a book on puppetry, built some puppets, and went back. "Now I am a puppeteer, will you hire me?" They did. Within a couple of years, he had his own show on that station, and the puppet that was to become Kermit the Frog was born. Throughout his career, my dad had to sell people on his ideas. He was determined to get his projects made and show the world what he could do. His character Dr. Teeth of The Electric Mayhem Band sings a song that says, "You can't take no for an answer." He rarely did.

Jim loved working collaboratively with other people. Work was play, and he loved a good game. He brought together writers, producers, puppeteers, and friends to make his productions happen. He was not unlike Kermit leading the Muppet gang to Hollywood in the first Muppet Movie when he says, "I've got a dream too, but it's about singing and dancing and making people happy. That's the kind of dream that gets better the more people you share it with." My dad was excited by the creative process and believed that with the right team he could accomplish anything. That attitude explains the third chapter, "Together We'll Nab It," featuring the voices of people who worked closely with Jim as they talk about what made his style of leadership special.

"It Starts When We're Kids," the fourth chapter, taps into my dad's childhood dreams and the imagination that made those dreams possible. Jim always had respect for children, and so his characters never talked down to them. When he started on *Sesame Street*, he had four kids of his own under the age of six, giving him plenty of firsthand experience with how thoughtful, emotional, and mischievous real children could be. When we were young, he enjoyed hearing the stories that we made up and encouraged us to explore the worlds of our imaginations. As we grew, he helped us to gain the skills to create on our own. As a parent and an artist, Jim truly embraced the energy and spontaneity of childhood. I don't think he ever lost the sense of wonder and appetite for discovery that we associate with kids.

The last chapter is called "A Part of Everything and Everyone." This is how Jim remembers feeling in one of his happiest moments of inspiration, lying under a big old tree in California. Dad always admired trees. As a young man, he often painted and drew them. He loved the variety of their shapes and the personalities they resembled. He enjoyed their age and elegance. In this chapter, he talks about nature and how intriguing it was for him to use our world as inspiration to create new worlds like those of *The Dark Crystal* and *Fraggle Rock*. He was also interested in the real world and wanted to do his part to make it better. He realized his limitations in this regard, but he never lost his faith that each act of kindness, each bit of understanding, and each smile can make a difference.

Compiling the quotes for this book has been a great pleasure for me. Reading the beautiful things that people have said about my father, looking through the letters that he wrote and the notes that he made, have brought me closer to him and to his way of thinking. It has given me great joy to have the words to the songs that he sang buzzing through my head as I go through my day.

Looking through his writings, I was struck by the honesty of a few simple lines on the first page of one notebook:

Beginning this is the hardest thing—I bought this book last week—I've wanted to do this for several months but there's something awesome about a totally blank book—and so beautiful—at least at this point it is.

My life is basically a very fortunate one and I first of all have no big complaints.

Writing did not always come easily to my father. He thought more in images and ideas than he did in words. He found the blank white page of the notebook both beautiful and awesome. It represented the infinite potential of yet another creative project. He started with a note of gratitude.

My dad's life was full of blessings. The unique way he approached life made it possible for him to create some of the most beloved characters the world has known and to use them to spread social values that were important to him, such as inclusiveness, tolerance, humor, and kindness. This book is intended to convey the many facets of my dad's being and his thinking. I hope you enjoy it.

—*Cheryl Henson*

8

Listen to Your Heart

I believe that we form our own lives, that we create our own reality, and that everything works out for the best. I know I drive some people crazy with what seems to be ridiculous optimism, but it has always worked out for me.

—Jim

*T*he words say, "It's not easy being green," but the song is about knowing who you are. And in it you hear Jim's message most clearly. He believed that people are good and that they want to do their best and that no matter how or why we might be different from anybody else, we should learn to love who we are and be proud of it.

—*Ray Charles*

*I*t's not that easy bein' green
Having to spend each day the color of the leaves,
When I think it might be nicer being red, or yellow,
    or gold
Or something much more colorful like that

It's not easy bein' green
It seems you blend in with so many other
    ordinary things
And people tend to pass you over,
'cause you're not standing out like flashy sparkles
    on the water,
or stars in the sky

But green is the color of spring
And green can be cool and friendly like
And green can be big like an ocean
Or important like a mountain
Or tall like a tree

When green is all there is to be,
It could make you wonder why.
But why wonder, why wonder?
I am green, and it'll do fine
And I think it's what I want to be

—Kermit

15

I don't know exactly where ideas come from, but when I'm working well ideas just appear. I've heard other people say similar things—so it's one of the ways I know there's help and guidance out there. It's just a matter of our figuring out how to receive the ideas or information that are waiting to be heard.

—*Jim*

*L*istening is the first step and the last step.

—*Cantus Fraggle*

*J*im was a dreamer… but he was pragmatic enough to make the dream happen. He was just absolutely determined to do that. There were certainly elements of both. But a dreamer was what he really was.

—*Jerry Juhl*

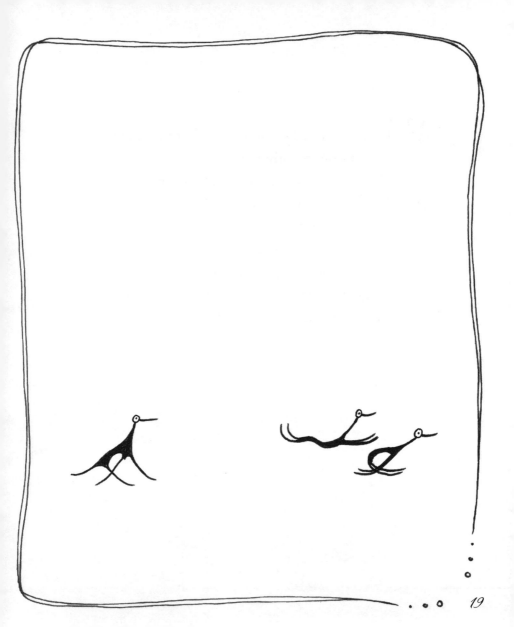

19

Why are there so many songs about rainbows,
And what's on the other side?
Rainbows are visions, but only illusions,
And rainbows have nothing to hide.
So we've been told
And some choose to believe it.

I know they're wrong, wait and see.
Someday we'll find it, the rainbow connection,
The lovers, the dreamers, and me.

Who said that every wish
    would be heard and answered,
When wished on the morning star.
Somebody thought of that, and someone believed it.
Look what it's done so far.
What's so amazing that keeps us stargazing,
And what do we think we might see?
Someday we'll find it, the rainbow connection,
The lovers, the dreamers, and me.

—Kermit

A LIST OF GOOD THINGS
ABOUT BEING A FROG

Being green

Sitting in the sun on a lily pad

Having thousands of brothers and sisters

Going to the hop

Playing leapfrog

Having bears and pigs and dogs and chickens as
your friends

Getting kissed by princesses hoping to turn you
into a handsome prince

—Kermit

Over the years, television has produced a few individuals blessed with the ability to touch our hearts, our minds, and our lives with their vision. It's not so much that these special people march to a different drummer, but that they carry their own orchestras around with them in their heads. And when we allow them to play their tunes, the sound reverberates for generations. They make us think and they make us laugh.

—*Candice Bergen*

Here in the middle of imagination, right in the
  middle of my head
I close my eyes and my room's not my room, and
  my bed isn't really my bed.
I look inside and discover things that are sometimes
  strange and new
And the most remarkable thoughts I think have a
  way of being true.

Here in the middle of imagination, right in the
  middle of my mind
I close my eyes and the night isn't dark and the
  things that I lose, I find.
Time stands still and the night is clear and the wind
  is warm and fair.
And the nicest place is the middle of imagination
  when I'm there.

—Ernie

As I try to zero in on what's important for the Muppets, I think it's a sense of innocence, naïveté —you know, the experience of a simple person meeting life. Even the most worldly of our characters is innocent. Our villains are innocent, really. And it's that innocence that I think is the connection to the audience.

—*Jim*

Simple is good.

—*Jim*

We always used to kid Jim that after telling everybody "simple is good," he would turn around and try to produce the most complicated work in the world and just about wipe out all of us—him most of all—in the process.

—*Jerry Juhl*

*J*im inspired people to be better than they thought
they could be. To be more creative, more daring,
more outrageous, and ultimately more successful.
And he did it all without raising his voice.

—*Bernie Brillstein*

29

*I*f just one person believes in you
Deep enough and strong enough
Believes in you hard enough and long enough
Before you knew it, someone else would think
"If he can do it, I can do it"
Making it two. Two whole people who believe
in you.
And maybe even you can believe in you too.

—*Robin and the Muppet Gang*

When I hear the art of puppetry discussed, I often feel frustrated in that it's one of those pure things that somehow becomes much less interesting when it is overdiscussed or analyzed. I feel it does what it does and even is a bit weakened if you know what it is doing. At its best, it is talking to a deeper part of you, and if you know that it's doing that, or you become aware of it, you lessen the ability to go straight in. Fairy tales certainly are in this category, as is a lot of fantasy—maybe everything is.

—*Jim*

I see Jim's life as a very Zen kind of thing. I never heard him say rude or bad things about other people. He lived, I think, by example. To show other people how to be by who you are.

—Jerry Nelson

*I*t's in every one of us to be wise
Find your heart, open up both your eyes
We can all know everything
Without ever knowing why
It's in every one of us by and by.

—*John Denver and the Muppets*

*J*im didn't tell you what to do. He just was. And by
him being what he was, he led and he taught. But
by not answering, sometimes you answered your
own question, and you could do more than you
thought you could.

—Frank Oz

I think there are lots of ways of leading very good lives and growing spiritually. This process of growth goes on whether we believe in it or not.

—Jim

Despite this discussion of things spiritual—I still think of myself as a very "human" being. I have the full complement of weaknesses, fears, problems, ego, and sensuality. But I think this is why we're here—to work our way through all this, and, hopefully, come out a bit wiser and better for having gone through it all.

—Jim

*J*im had a sense of humor that just sorted out life. And, you know, too much of life for most people is involved in picking what are really fairly petty things and turning them into deep tragedies and horrible melodramas. And Jim always cut through that.

—Jerry Juhl

I wish I had a coat of silk
   the color of the sky.
I wish I had a lady
   fair as any butterfly.
I wish I had a house of stone
   that looks down on the sea.
But most of all I wish
   that I was someone else but me.

Kermit: Hi there Gonzo—what a lovely
   place this is!
Gonzo: Yeah.
Kermit: What's the matter?
Gonzo: I don't have a coat of silk
Kermit: But still you have the sky.
Gonzo: I don't have a lady
Kermit: But there goes a butterfly.

Now I don't have a house of stone
    but I can see the sea.
Now most of all I guess
That I am happy to be me.
…I'm happy to be me.

— *Gonzo*

41

Music was always an important element in Jim's work. He employed music not only as a means to further his comic purposes, but also as a way of expressing his gentleness and the vulnerability hidden in his heart.

—*Joan Ganz Cooney*

*S*ometimes I have trouble falling asleep but it's not
  so bad
I don't worry and I don't weep. In fact I'm glad.

Because I get up off my pillow and I flip on the
  light.
I get down and get hip in the still of the night
I stretch and I yawn and then I breathe real deep
And dance myself to sleep.

I hoof around my beddie just a-tappin' my toes
Before I know what's happened I'm a-ready to doze
Got some partners I can count on called the boogie-
  woogie sheep
I dance myself to sleep.

—Ernie

I spend a few minutes in meditation and prayer each morning. I find that this really helps me to start the day with a good frame of reference. As part of my prayers, I thank whoever is helping me—I'm sure somebody or something is—I express gratitude for all my blessings and I try to forgive the people that I'm feeling negative toward. I try hard not to judge anyone, and I try to bless everyone who is a part of my life, particularly anyone with whom I am having any problems.

—*Jim*

W̲e *see* with our eyes. We *know* with our hearts.
Outside…Inside.

—*Cantus Fraggle*

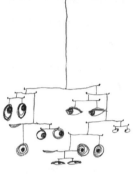

*T*here are places that contain you,
There are corners in your soul,
There are plastic laminations
In your life.
But when you're on the inside
Of the outside of your thought,
Do they restrain,
Or do you stay yourself?

Now the inside of the near place
Is outside of the far,
But you can only face your space one way.
You're really in the middle
Of the inside of yourself.

—*Guitarist from "The Cube," 1969*

But, you've heard enough. Now, it's time for you to listen. Go and find your songs.

—*Cantus Fraggle*

Dynamite Determination

My name is Jim Henson and I am a puppeteer.
I'm called a puppeteer because I do puppets.
There are all different kinds of puppets…
There have been puppets almost as long as there
   have been people.

One of the nice things about puppets is that it's
   your own hand in there.
You can make it do anything you want it to.

—Jim

I cannot say why I am good at what I do, but I can say that I work very hard at it. Nor am I aware of any conscious career decisions. I've always found that one thing leads to another, and that I've moved from project to project in a natural progression.

Perhaps one thing that has helped me in achieving my goals is that I sincerely believe in what I do, and get great pleasure from it. I feel very fortunate because I can do what I love to do.

—Jim

Whenever there's a dream worth a-dreamin'
And you want to see that dream come true
There'll be plenty people talkin',
Say forget all about it
Say it isn't worth all the trouble,
All the trouble that you're goin' through
Well, what can you do?

You can't take no for an answer
You can't take no for an answer
You can't take no for an answer.
No, no, no!

Whatcha gonna do when the times get tough,
And the world's treatin' you unkind?
You've got to hang on to your optimistic outlook,
And keep possession of your positive state of mind.

—Dr. Teeth

Many of the things I've done in my life have basically been self-taught. I think we, as the Muppets, broke new ground because we approached puppetry from a different angle. I had never worked with puppets when I was a kid, and even when I began on television, I really didn't know what I was doing. I'm sure that this was a good thing, because I learned as I tackled each problem. I think if you study—if you learn too much of what others have done, you may tend to take the same direction as everybody else.

—Jim

There are no rules, and those are the rules.

—Cantus Fraggle

*D*on't care what they say, 'cause I know where to
   find my way,
It won't be the way they said to go.

But I'm not like they say, I just want to find
   my way,
I'm goin' the way I've got to go.

So show me a way to go and I'll go free, I hope
   you'll see
That I'm goin' the way I've got to go.

—Cotterpin Doozer

*J*im inspired people to do huge amounts of work; more work, and better work, than they thought they were capable of. And he did that by pushing himself. He was very close to us all. We all worked closely together. We all watched him. And year after year we watched him push himself beyond what we could possibly imagine. You had to try to keep up with the guy—it seemed only fair.

—Jerry Juhl

I don't resent working long hours. I shouldn't — I'm the one who set up my life this way. I love to work. It's the thing that I get the most satisfaction out of — and probably what I do best. Not that I don't enjoy days off. I love vacations and loafing around. But I think much of the world has the wrong idea of working. It's one of the good things in life. The feeling of accomplishment is more real and satisfying than finishing a good meal — or looking at one's accumulated wealth.

—Jim

I guess I was wrong when I said I never promised anyone. I promised me.

—*Kermit*

Kermit is the eye in the middle of the hurricane. And, you know, he's always in control. Sometimes just barely, but he's always in control. And the interesting thing about it, of course, is that he created the hurricane.

—*Jerry Juhl*

*L*ook at all those people out there. Lots of people. But my friends…my friends are all gone. Well, I'm, I'm going to get 'em back. I'm gonna get 'em back! 'Cause the show's not dead as long as I believe in it. And I'm gonna sell that show. And we're all gonna be on Broadway. You hear me, New York? We're gonna be on Broadway! Because, because I'm not giving up! I'm still here and I'm stayin'! You hear that, New York? I'm stayin' here. The frog is stayin'.

—*Kermit*

I've discovered that homework assignments aren't much different from work assignments in the grownup world. That's whether you're a farmer or a man who makes Muppet productions. With homework you've got spelling, math, and history. A farmer has peas, beans, and corn to grow. A Muppet man has *Fraggle Rock*, *The Muppets Take Manhattan*, and a whole lot of upcoming Muppet productions.

First you decide which job gets priority. Then you knuckle down and get to work. The more you stick with your plan and work at what you have to do, the more time you'll save for the things you love to do. It so happens that what I have to do is what I love to do. But since I know that isn't true for everyone, here's a secret: Once you've decided on priority, do the jobs you like least *first*! It makes each successive job easier.

If you care about what you do and work hard at it, there isn't anything you can't do if you want to.

—*Jim*

Well, when the path is steep and stony and the
    night is all around
And the way that you must take is far away
When your heart is lost and lonely and the map
    cannot be found
Here's a simple little spell that you can say:

You've got to face facts, act fast on your own
Preparation, perspiration, dynamite determination
Pack snacks, make tracks all alone
Don't be cute. Time to scoot. Head out to your
    destination.

Chase the future, face the great unknown.

—*Gobo Fraggle*

*A*ll those characters are part of Jim. The Swedish Chef and his goofiness was part of Jim. Kermit's sweetness and his simplicity and his strength, Jim was an extraordinarily strong human being. That came out in his characters.

—*Frank Oz*

*T*his frog has a song to be sung.
This frog isn't gonna spend his life in a swamp
Catchin' flies with his tongue.
This frog may slip and stumble,
But this frog tries again.
This frog will never grumble,
But fall to rise again.
This frog is staying with it
Like a tick sticks to a dog.
I'm gonna win!
You're gonna love this frog!

—Kermit

When I was a tadpole there was really only one thing that I collected. I had a file of newspaper and magazine articles on Frogs in Show Business. It was a small collection, but I think it influenced me a lot.

—*Kermit*

You could be a coward, you could be a king
You could be the kind of kid who teaches us to sing
You could be whatever your little heart desires
You could be a walkin', talkin', breathin' ball of fire.

Sometimes a mountain, sometimes a stone
Sometimes a river windin' round to find a home
You could crawl away, you could fly higher
You could be a walkin' talkin' breathin' ball of fire.

—Cantus Fraggle

A driver was talking to me today asking, "Did you
ever, in your wildest dreams, think you would have
success like this?" The honest answer to this, which
I do occasionally admit, is that yes, I've always
known I would be very successful in anything I
decided to do—and it turned out to be puppetry.

—Jim

*A*nybody's lover, everybody's brother,
I wanna be your lifetime friend,
Crazy as a rocket, nothing in my pocket,
I keep it at the rainbow's end.
I never think of money; I think of milk and honey,
Grinnin' like a Cheshire cat.
I focus on the pleasure, something I can treasure.
Can you picture that?

Fact is, there's nothing out there you can't do.
Yeah, even Santa Claus believes in you.
Beat down the walls,
Begin, believe, behold, begat.
Be a better drummer; be an up-an'-comer.
Can you picture that?!

—*Dr. Teeth & the Electric Mayhem*

Together We'll Nab It

I love my work, and because I enjoy it, it doesn't really feel like work. Thus I spend most of my time working. I like working collaboratively with people. At its best, the film and television world functions creatively this way. I have a terrific group of people who work with me, and I think of the work that we do as "our" work.

—*Jim*

Yeah, well, I've got a dream too. But it's about
singing and dancing and making people happy.
That's the kind of dream that gets better the more
people you share it with. And, well, I've found a
whole bunch of friends who have the same dream.
And it kind of makes us like a family.

—*Kermit*

*O*ur group of performers has been together for many years and we know each other so well that we can kind of bounce off each other when we're working together. This working relationship has a kind of marvelous chemistry to it. I think it's terribly important that, when we're working in the studio, we work with this kind of affection and high spirits.

—Jim

*T*he game on *The Muppet Show* was to upstage as much as you could. Jim loved upstaging and he would reward you for it. I remember during the instrumental break on a production number featuring Miss Piggy, I had my character lean over the balcony backwards and play a trumpet solo upside down, and Jim was in hysterics. It was great to have a boss who really sanctioned and encouraged anarchy.

—*Dave Goelz*

*C*ertainly we look for creativity and a sense of humor, people who have a positive view of the world, that kind of thing. We look for people that work collaboratively. It's not just me doing this stuff, it's a lot of us creating it, writers and designers and puppeteers. We have a good time working together too.

—*Jim*

Kermit's function on this show is very much like my own in that he's trying to hold together this group of crazies. And that's not unlike what I do.

—*Jim*

*J*im was a master collaborator, not just because he allowed equal time for everyone's input, but because he had the ability to validate that input and rank its usefulness at the same time. From big projects to individual scenes, Jim presented a group of carefully selected people with his vision and allowed us all to expand and evolve that vision. He allowed for everyone to be right, but he knew everyone couldn't be equally right.

—*Steve Whitmire*

*C*reatively, I find I work best if I can work with someone—talking things over as ideas come up. I do this best with people I'm very comfortable with—there has to be an absolutely pressure-free situation for this to work well. Jerry Juhl and I have always been able to work this way. It's important to be able to say virtually anything—which may be totally silly or stupid or obscene—in a no-risk situation.

—Jim

*J*im was the fellow who uncorked the bottle, you
know. He not only uncorked the bottle, he also
shook it up.

—*Frank Oz*

One of the things that I think television allows you to do a bit more than film is to work a little more spontaneously. In television, things will happen because you're working very fast and because it's easy. Tape is rolling and you try several different kinds of things. With film, particularly if you do a big expensive movie, by the time you're shooting it, you've been on the script for years. You've examined every little line and you don't even know if it's funny anymore. Comedy through this whole process is very difficult. Everything is zeroed down and you know exactly what you're going to shoot. You have to break from that and consciously try not to get yourself locked into that way of thinking.

—Jim

A film is not done by one person. It's done by a lot of people. I love this whole collaborative aspect. When it works well, you end up with something better than any of us started out to do.

—Jim

I guess I learned everything from my father. There was guidance from him throughout. He taught me to identify a person's talent, nurture that talent, and encourage them to look to themselves for solutions. That's probably what he taught me more than anything—a mind-set, a work ethic.

—*Brian Henson*

*D*ance your cares away, worry's for another day.
Let the Music play down at Fraggle Rock.
Work your cares away, dancing's for another day.
Work your cares away down at Fraggle Rock.

— *The Fraggles*

THE
MUPPET MACHINE

We are primarily a company of creative people, whose art we are helping to bring to the world. At the same time, we recognize that business enables art "to happen," and that business plays an essential role in communicating art to a broad audience. As both artists and businesspersons, we understand the value of both worlds, and so we bring them together in a way that facilitates the realization of our artistic vision.

—Jim

Bert: I like paper clips.

Ernie: Paper clips?

Bert: Paper clips! I like bottle caps.

Ernie: Bottle caps?

Bert: Bottle caps! I love pigeons, yeah!

Ernie: Pigeons?

Bert: Love pigeons. Oh, yes, I do!

Ernie: Well, Bert, you know, I don't really like any
of those things, but I like you!

Bert: Aw, Ernie.

Ernie: I like playing jokes.

Bert: Playing jokes?

Ernie: Playing jokes! Love my rubber duck.

Bert: Rubber duck?

Ernie: Rubber Duckie! I like bubble gum.

Bert: Bubble gum?

Ernie: Bubble gum, yes, I do!

Bert: Well, now, Ernie, I'm not crazy 'bout any of
those things, but I like you!

Ernie: I like to lie awake in bed at night and talk
to you.

Bert: Yeah, I know. I like to say good night and
go to sleep!

Ernie: I like to go and see the big hippopotamus in
the zoo.

Bert: Hey, Ernie, you know what?

Ernie: What, Bert?

Bert: I like that too!

Ernie: I like jelly beans.

Bert: Jelly beans?

Ernie: Jelly beans!

Bert: I like lentil soup.

Ernie: Lentil soup?

Bert: Yeah! I like a marching band.

Ernie: I like a music box.

Both: Yes, I do!

Ernie: But though I don't always like everything...

Bert: That I like,

Both: Still I like you!

Bert: Though I'm not too crazy 'bout your Rubber
Duckie,

Ernie: Though I don't love pigeons, still we're
awfully lucky,

Both: 'Cause I like you!

*J*im was an extraordinary human being—kind, patient, a natural leader, open to other people's ideas, and also open to different ways of thinking and philosophies. He was a truly gentle man. He treated everyone the same whether they were the head of the network or the fellow who emptied the trash. He also *loved* what he did, and when you made him laugh it felt like Christmas. I was very lucky to have known him since I was the first female puppeteer he hired on the show. I learned not only how to puppeteer but how to be a good human being. He set a wonderful example.

—*Fran Brill*

There is a sense of our characters caring for each other and having respect for each other. A positive feeling. A positive view of life. That's a key to everything we do. I believe that everything we do should have part of that. Sometimes we're too heavy in terms of ourselves and trying to carry an idea, and telling kids what life is about. I often have to tell myself that too.

—*Jim*

Whenever characters become self-important or sentimental in the Muppets, then there's always another character there to blow them up immediately.

—Frank Oz

*I*n a company, the mannerisms and standards of the boss trickle down. Jim always let us shine. He never demanded—he knew we wanted to give 110%. He was the example and we wanted to be as creative and hardworking as he was. He always used praise. He never had to tell us when it wasn't going well. We knew it and we'd work hard at turning it around. He was our inspiration. Still is.

—*Kevin Clash*

*J*im always said that you are where you are because that's where you need to be; and if you need to move on, you will move on. He was very generous. He said, "Well, I know that this is what you need to do. And we're not going to lose touch." We never did. I returned to work with him on several projects. He was not worried that people went off to do their own thing, because he knew that other people were coming in. He felt it was really important to have fresh, new ideas.

—*Bonnie Erickson*

Moving right along
In search of good times
And good news,
With good friends you can't lose.
This could become a habit.

Opportunity just knocked,
Let's reach out and grab it,
Together we'll nab it,
We'll hitch-hike, bus, or yellow cab it.

—Kermit and Fozzie

A good character is almost always derived from an aspect of the performer's personality. That is true for all the Muppet performers, including Jim. Jim's characters Ernie, the Swedish Chef, Dr. Teeth, Rowlf the Dog, Guy Smiley, and Convincing John were all part of him, but none more so than Kermit, who occupied the exact same relationship to the *Muppet Show* characters as Jim did to his employees.

—*Dave Goelz*

Jim was a creatively selfless and a completely generous person—always most impressed not with his own work but with the work of the people around him. He loved watching people from different disciplines put their heads together to solve a complicated problem.

—*Brian Henson*

I loved the way Don Sahlin played. Throughout his life Don would play—pick up some bit of feathers and attach a long rubber band to it—stretch it down the hall, and release it as you came into the room, or take some half-formed puppet and put a ridiculous hat on it, or pose it in the john. He had this sense of playfulness that he actually used—and inspiration would come out of those moments. He would also let a problem mull around in the back of his head— waiting for his "muse" to find the solution. Many great solutions came this way!

—*Jim*

Wake up in the morning
Get yourself to work.
Fraggles never fool around.
Fraggles never shirk.
Your duty's always waiting
And duty must be done.
There's Ping-Pong games that must be played
And songs that must be sung.

—*Gobo and the Fraggles*

It Starts When We're Kids

When I was young, my ambition was to be one of the people who made a difference in this world. My hope still is to leave the world a little bit better for my having been here.

It's a wonderful life and I love it.

—*Jim*

*I*t starts when we're kids, a show-off in school;
Makin' faces at friends, you're a clown and a fool.
Doin' pratfalls and birdcalls and bad imitations;
Ignoring your homework, now that's dedication.
You work to the mirror, you're getting standing
    ovations.
You're burning with hope, you're building up steam.
What was once juvenilish is grown-up and stylish,
You're close to your dream.
Then somebody out there loves you,
Stands up and hollers for more;
You found a home at the Magic Store.

— The Muppets

*A*s children, we all live in a world of imagination, of fantasy, and for some of us that world of make-believe continues into adulthood. Certainly I've lived my whole life through my imagination. But the world of imagination is there for all of us—a sense of play, of pretending, of wonder. It's there with us as we live.

—*Jim*

Well, I'd like to visit the moon
On a rocket ship high in the air
Yes, I'd like to visit the moon
But I don't think I'd like to live there.

Though I'd like to look down at the earth
   from above
Soon I'd miss all the places and people I love
So although I might like it for one afternoon
I don't want to live on the moon.

I'd like to travel under the sea
I could meet all the fish everywhere
Yes I'd travel under the sea
But I don't think I'd like to live there.

I might stay for a day there if I had my wish
But there's not much to do when your friends
   are all fish
And an oyster and clam aren't real family
So I don't want to live in the sea.

So if I should visit the moon
Well I'll dance on a moonbeam and then
I will make a wish on a star
And I'll wish I was home once again.

—Ernie

I believe that we can use television and film to be an influence for good; that we can help to shape the thoughts of children and adults in a positive way. As it turned out, I am very proud of some of the work we've done, and I think we can do many more good things.

—Jim

Jim was intrigued with his children. The way they heard things. The way they listened to things. The way they got up every day and every day was a new adventure, a new challenge. They were ready to see everything. They had a great sense of humor and so he immediately started using them to find out what was funny, what worked. He really respected their opinions.

—*Jane Henson*

A child's use of imagination and fantasy blends into his use of creativity. The child can use his imagination to try out whole new directions. There are many ways of doing something. Look for what no one has tried before; go back and question one or more of the basic "givens" of a situation.

—Jim

I've found that children keep their imaginations a lot longer than parents think they do. Parents are concerned that if kids see that a person operates the Muppet, an illusion will be shattered. But I think kids see us as just the people who carry their friends around.

—*Kevin Clash*

When I was a child, my mother's family would gather at my grandmother's house. Fifteen or twenty people would be there, sitting around the dinner table, and my grandparents would have stories to tell—usually stories from their childhood. They would tell a tale, and somebody would try to top it. I've always felt that these childhood experiences of my family sitting around the dinner table, making each other laugh, were my introduction to humor.

—*Jim*

The attitude you have as a parent is what your kids will learn from more than what you tell them. They don't remember what you try to teach them.

They remember what you are.

—*Jim*

*H*ere's some simple advice: Always be yourself. Never take yourself too seriously. And beware of advice from experts, pigs, and members of Parliament.

—*Kermit*

*A*s children, we were all invited into his world, into his work, to share and even to help create. He thought it all belonged together; work and family, kids and adults, fun and projects. Everything was a project, whether it was a piece of painted furniture for the playroom, a special homemade Christmas ornament, or a treatment for a network television show. In my memory, it all blended together as a constant outpouring of creativity.

—*Lisa Henson*

From my own point of view, I can only tell you what has worked for me—find something you really enjoy doing and pursue it. For me it was artwork. Since other subjects came to me with more difficulty, I tried to combine art with them. So, for example, in history, I would often provide drawings depicting a particular period or situation—bringing together both cultural and historical elements. It did not necessarily bring up my history grade, but it did keep my mind open to history as it related to something I loved.

—*Jim*

Be proud of your flippers
And the flies that you catch
And the logs that you leap
And the eggs you will hatch.
We're under the stars
And we're smaller than men
But I'm proud to be one of the frogs in the glen.

—*Kermit*

I was about seventeen when I first started building puppets and working on television. For a long time, it was just something to do to go through college, paying my way through school. Then very slowly I realized that this was something a grown man could do for a living. Most people, and particularly kids, don't realize that they are in control of their lives and they're the ones that are going to make the decisions and they're the ones that are going to actually make it one way or the other.

Usually adolescence is a time when kids feel that the world is doing it to them, whether it's their parents doing it to them or their teachers doing it or their other friends doing it to them, and that they are the victim of all of this. Somewhere in here, you have to learn that you're not the victim, but instead you're the one that's doing it. That moment is sometimes a long slow realization or sometimes it's turning on a light switch. All of a sudden you realize that you are the person who has control of your life.

—Jim

*T*he most sophisticated people I know—inside they're all children. We never really lose a certain sense we had when we were kids.

—Jim

Ernie: Hey, Bert.

Bert: What is it, Ernie?

Ernie: You know, Bert, I just remembered I didn't put away all my toys. I left a big mess in the other room. Do you think I should get up and clean that stuff up now?

Bert: Ernie, it's time to go to sleep now. You can do that in the morning.

Ernie: It's pretty messy in there, Bert.

Bert: Well, Ernie, you're just a little messy. I've learned that. I'm used to it. Let's go to sleep.

Ernie: You know, Bert, you're a real friend. I'm messy and you don't like it messy, but because I'm your friend, you don't mind too much if I'm messy.

Bert: Well, not too much, Ernie. Let's just go to sleep.

Ernie: But that's what a friend is, Bert. I mean, not minding too much because you like someone. That's a friend, Bert. A pal. Not minding, that's what friends are for!

I feel that almost everyone maintains a childlike quality throughout their adulthood. One of the nice things about the puppet form is that it has the ability to communicate with this childlike side of the audience. The personalities of the Muppet characters are really quite innocent and everyone, in some way or another, seems to be able to relate to this innocence.

—Jim

I believe that life is basically a process of growth —that we go through many lives, choosing those situations and problems that we will learn through.

—*Jim*

*T*adpole, wiggling in the water,
Brand new world is there for you to see.
Lots of time till you grow up to be
A big frog like me.

Tadpole, haven't got a worry,
Biggest job is swimming peacefully.
Wonder if you know you'll grow up to be
A big frog like me.

Changes happen as time passes by.
Soon enough, you'll be grown,
With a home on a lily pad
And some tadpoles of your own.

Oh, little tadpole, wiggling in the water
Far from all responsibility.
Take your time till you grow up to be
A big frog like me.
Tadpole, take your time to be
A big, green, grown-up frog like me.

—Kermit

*A*t home we had all kinds of things going on all the time. All kinds of creative things going on. So if there were puppets, they were made in the kitchen out of wooden spoons and paper cups and things like that. People were dressing up and making things all the time. Just a general feeling of creativity was always around the house.

—*Jane Henson*

No time is wasted time.

—*Cantus Fraggle*

*J*im had five children of his own, and by nature was extremely playful. He related well to children because he could access that part of himself. The fascinating thing was that while he functioned as an astute businessman, he could integrate play into the process.

I now have children of my own, and have come to believe we are all born perfect—well, maybe not absolutely perfect, but certainly completely without evil. As a parent, one of my goals is to see whether I can raise my children to survive in the world without losing that childlike innocence, trust, optimism, curiosity, and decency. I am certain it is possible because Jim was the living embodiment of it.

—Dave Goelz

*L*ike a baby when it is sleeping
In its loving mother's arms
What a newborn baby dreams is a mystery.

But his life will find a purpose
And in time he'll understand
When the river meets the sea.

—*Ma Otter*

I really do believe that all of you are at the beginning of a wonderful journey. As you start traveling down that road of life, remember this: There are never enough comfort stops. The places you're going to are never on the map. And once you get that map out, you won't be able to refold it no matter how smart you are.

So forget the map, roll down the windows, and whenever you can, pull over and have a picnic with a pig. And if you can help it, never fly as cargo.

—*Kermit*

*L*ife is meant to be fun, and joyous, and fulfilling. May each of yours be that—having each of you as a child of mine has certainly been one of the good things in my life. Know that I've always loved each of you with an eternal, bottomless love. A love that has nothing to do with each other, for I feel my love for each of you is total and all-encompassing.

Please watch out for each other and love and forgive everybody. It's a good life, enjoy it.

—Jim

A Part of Everything and Everyone

I believe in taking a positive attitude toward the world, toward people, and toward my work. I think I'm here for a purpose. I think it's likely that we all are, but I'm only sure about myself. I try to tune myself in to whatever it is that I'm supposed to be, and I try to think of myself as a part of all of us — all mankind and all life. I find it's not easy to keep these lofty thoughts in mind as the day goes by, but it certainly helps me a great deal to start out this way.

—Jim

Many people see Jim as an extraordinary creator and I realize that I see Jim first as an appreciator. He appreciated so much. He loved London. He loved walking on the heath. He loved Parliament Hill, flying kites. He appreciated his family and his colleagues and his Muppet family and he appreciated the performance and the design of a puppet. He appreciated the detail on a Persian rug. He appreciated beauty. I really don't believe that Jim could have been such an extraordinary creator if he hadn't been such an extraordinary appreciator.

—*Frank Oz*

I find that it's very important for me to stop every now and then and get recharged and reinspired. The beauty of nature has been one of the great inspirations in my life. Growing up as an artist, I've always been in awe of the incredible beauty of every last bit of design in nature. The wonderful color schemes of nature that always work harmoniously are particularly dazzling to me. I love to lie in an open field looking up at the sky. One of my happiest moments of inspiration came to me many years ago as I lay on the grass, looking up into the leaves and branches of a big old tree in California. I remember feeling very much a part of everything and everyone.

—*Jim*

*H*ave you ever noticed
Clouds can look like fluffy pillows?
Have you ever counted all the stars up in the sky?
Have you ever watched the birds fly by?

Take a look above you.
Squirrels scurry up an oak tree.
See that yellow circle?
That's the sun who gives us light.
Way up high, I think I see a kite.

I wonder 'bout the world above
Up there.
No matter where you go, it's everywhere.

Now the sun is setting,
Getting ready for tomorrow.
Soon the moon'll be glowing,
Showing off the moonlight.
Take a look above you,
Discover the view.
If you haven't noticed,
Please do. Please do. Please do.

—Kermit

*H*e didn't have much time for quiet contemplation, but he took it wherever he could. He could stretch out a moment, looking out at the nice weather from his window above Central Park, and you knew he was really aware. Sometimes he expressed the desire for a simpler life, like when he admired the job of the man who walks along the road picking up trash with a long stick. He thought that guy had a great job, walking along with a stick (my father loved walking sticks), enjoying the road, and doing only good in the world, with hundreds of small actions.

—*Lisa Henson*

When the week is finally over,
It is wonderful to go
And putter in my garden
Where I watch the flowers grow.

It is pleasant in my garden
As I cultivate my seeds;
I plant and hoe and water
And I clear away the weeds.

Though it's frantic at the theater,
Here I leave that all behind,
And the calm within my garden
Gives this frog some peace of mind.

—*Kermit*

What a thrill. Two days at the Cannes Film
Festival. Lord Grade's office chartered a flight to
take Jim and me to France. Two fabulous suites
awaited us, a detailed itinerary as well as a major
dinner reservation. The following day at the festival
was loaded with special events and screenings. Our
movies and *The Muppet Show* were at the peak of
their popularity around the world and Jim was
showered with praise and adoration. The evening
ended with a party on a private yacht loaded with
stars and movers and shakers. We left the yacht at
one o'clock in the morning and walked along the
dock. Even the moon seemed to do a shimmer dance
on the water just for Jim. He was mesmerized by
the beauty, the serenity, and the nurturing power
of Nature. None of the glitz of Cannes or all the
accolades he received had this effect on him.

—*David Lazer*

*S*how me the light in a butterfly's eye
And show me the dreams of the earth and the sky

Show me the night, show me the day
Show me the secret that dances away
There's a rainbow I wish I could climb like a tree
A bug and a boulder that beckon to me
Show me leaves in the spring
Show me love on the wing
Show me things that I long to explore
Show me more.

—*Mokey Fraggle*

Working as I do with movement of puppet creatures, I'm always struck by the feebleness of our efforts to achieve naturalistic movement. Just looking at the incredible movement of a lizard or a bird, or even the smallest insect, can be a very humbling experience.

—Jim

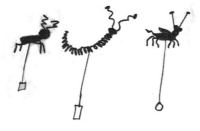

I have a lot of great memories from the swamp. I remember when I was little, we'd all just sit out on our lily pads for hours and hours, rocking gently on the water and listening to the soft, sweet sound of chirping crickets…Then, of course, we'd eat the crickets…but that's another story.

—*Kermit*

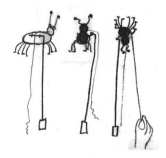

*U*nderneath the zaniness, or perhaps standing next to it, there was a sense of decency that the characters had, about the world and to each other. And I think that's one of the real legacies that Jim left. And I think it's one of the reasons he's so loved today, because he could be a pop culture figure doing mass entertainment, and he could explore the edges of crazy, goofy comedy. But at the core, there was always a sense of social values and decency.

—*Jerry Juhl*

If our "message" is anything, it's a positive approach to life. That life is basically good. People are basically good.

—*Jim*

*J*im didn't think in terms of boundaries at all the way the rest of us do. There are always these fences we build around ourselves and our ideas. Jim seemed to have no fences.

—Jon Stone

*J*im wanted to make a difference. He was brave enough to be able to say, "I want to do a show that brings peace to the world, and I want us all to sit down and talk about it." He knew that television shows do not bring peace to the world, but he was not so cynical as to say we can't think about it. There was a kind of idealism there that could seem naïve and childlike, but that didn't mean that it couldn't come true.

—*Jerry Juhl*

What the show is really about is people getting along with other people, and understanding the delicate balances of the natural world.

The world of the Fraggles will have its own natural balances, although these will be rather insane. But still we will make the point that everything affects everything else, and that there is a beauty and harmony of life to be appreciated.

These are topics that can be dealt with in a symbolic way, which is what puppets basically do all the time. These are also two of the areas that children in the next generation or so will have to deal with in very real terms.

—Jim

*T*he goal of this show would be to get across the idea of a global community, to make the world a little smaller and friendlier for the viewers. Music seems like a good vehicle for expressing this, because even though people and their music differ in fascinating ways from country to country, people are still people.

—Jim

*S*ome say the world is getting too small
I say with kindness
There's room for us all
Our world is always changing
Every day's a surprise
Love can open your eyes
In our world

When night lays sad upon you
Go watch a laughing sunrise
Love can open your eyes
In our world

—*Ma Otter*

*I*t's such a wonderful challenge to try to design an entire world—new kinds of life, vegetation, etc., like no one has ever seen before.

I don't think anyone has made a film that looks like *The Dark Crystal*—so, as far as I'm concerned, we're breaking new ground—and that's always one of the most exciting things for me. I love to feel I'm doing something for the first time—or using puppets in a way that no one has either thought of—or ever been able to do.

—Jim

M any ages ago, in our arrogance and delusion
we shattered the pure Crystal, and our world
split apart.

Your courage and sacrifice have made us whole.
And restored the power of the Crystal.

Hold her to you.

She is part of you as we all are part of each other.

Now we leave you the Crystal of truth. Make your
world in its light.

—*urSkeks*, The Dark Crystal

I believe that my father had some kind of direct experience of the spiritual nature of reality, maybe a vision, that he tried to convey perhaps unconsciously in his work—that this world we experience is illusory and that there is a different, more loving and transcendent reality beyond this world of imagined conflicts.

—*Lisa Henson*

At some point in my life I decided, rightly or wrongly, that there are many situations in this life that I can't do much about: acts of terrorism, feelings of nationalistic prejudice, cold war, etc. So what I should do is concentrate on the situations that my energy can affect.

—*Jim*

This is the place and this is the time
To clear the heart and open the mind.

When you're weary with the world
And the storms in which you're whirled
You can reach out, feel the love, the joy
Feel the breeze and smell the grass
Hear the birds sing as they pass
Thru the branches of the trees, the joy

The world gives us love we can share
Replacing the woe and the care with joy.

—Mokey Fraggle

I know that it's easier to portray a world that's filled with cynicism and anger, where problems are solved with violence. That's titillating. It's an easy out. What's a whole lot tougher is to offer alternatives, to present other ways conflicts can be resolved, and to show that you can have a positive impact on your world. To do that, you have to put yourself out on a limb, take chances, and run the risk of being called a do-gooder.

—*Jim*

I'd love to see on *Sesame Street* a brief segment that relates to children all over the world. A piece that says that there are lots of different kinds of kids and worlds, but that beneath it all, we are all one family.

What I'm interested in is just having kids see other kids, other races, other cultures, in very different settings—all going through similar things. Global stuff.

—*Jim*

*U*nless you have moved among the peoples of
this earth, who have so little hope for the future of
their lives, you will never really understand how
Jim Henson has made a difference for them. Those
desperate places where parents watch their children grow, knowing they will never be educated,
who will never have a chance at life as it should be,
these same parents watch as Jim's creations for the
first time not only put smiles on the faces of their
children, but develop in them the appetite to learn
watching *Sesame Street*, and the ability to love
because they see the love and the caring that
exudes from the Muppets and the Henson family
of creatures.

—*Harry Belafonte*

All of this stuff is about mankind trying to see himself in perspective. That's what literature is about, that's what art is. It's trying to figure out what you are and what you're doing here. This is the kind of thing that puppetry does very well. It goes way back to when men first carved little wooden dolls of themselves and drew stick figures on cave walls. It's why kids like teddy bears and little girls like dolls. It's all one thing. Puppetry is part of the real raw essential elements of all that stuff.

—Jim

*S*ome of the early puppets were used by witch doctors or for religious purposes. Puppets have often been connected with magic. Certainly Edgar Bergen's work with Charlie McCarthy and Mortimer Snerd was magic, magic in the real sense. Something happened when Edgar spoke through Charlie, things were said that couldn't be said by ordinary people. It's a way of looking at ourselves and our world in a fresh perspective. That's what theater does and what humor does and what Edgar Bergen did. He left this world a happier place because he was here, and I think that's about the finest thing a person can do with his life.

—*Jim*

From Kermit the Frog, literally an extension of Jim, comes a life-affirming decency, a passionate belief that there are stories to tell which don't exclude children and don't insult adults, which don't exclude adults but which don't insult children, which can be outrageous and innovative without being arch or misanthropic. There's anarchy here, but it's anarchy that celebrates rather than destroys.

—*Anthony Minghella*

Yes, it's one of the basic truths of the physical universe, Sprocket. Things don't disappear. They just change, and change, and change again.

—*Doc, from* Fraggle Rock

When Jim left the planet so suddenly, all of us who loved him, worked with him, were inspired by him, gathered in New York City. We were like dandelion seeds clinging to the stem and to each other. And on May 16th, the wind began to blow.

There's no stem anymore. We're all floating on the breeze. And it's scary and exhilarating. And there's nothing we can do about it. But gradually, we'll all drift to the ground and plant ourselves. And no matter what we grow into, it'll be influenced by Jim. We're Jim's seeds. And it's not only those of us who knew him. Everyone who was touched by his work is a Jim-seed.

He changed our lives. He changed the world.
And we'll continue his work, because that's how
inspiration operates. People die, but inspiration
lives and grows. Inspired by his gentleness, we'll fill
the world with gentleness. Inspired by his vision,
we'll fill the world with vision. Inspired by his
chicken imitation, we'll fill the world with laughter.

—*Jocelyn Stevenson*

Life's like a movie, write your own ending
Keep believing, keep pretending
We've done just what we set out to do
Thanks to the lovers, the dreamers, and you.

—Kermit and the Muppets

Contributors

Jim Henson was born in Mississippi on September 24, 1936. Around 1947, the Henson family moved to Maryland, and Jim developed an intense interest in the new and exciting visual medium of television. In 1954, while still in high school, Jim began his television career performing puppets on a local Washington, D.C., Saturday morning program. The following year, as a freshman at the University of Maryland, he was given his own twice-daily, five-minute show, *Sam and Friends*, which he produced with fellow University of Maryland student Jane Nebel. They were married in 1959, and went on to have five children together. With *Sam and Friends*, Jim and Jane created a distinct Muppet style with snarky humor and innovative technical tricks.

The success of *Sam and Friends* led to guest appearances on a number of national network programs. Jim also began making hundreds of humorous commercials for sponsors throughout the country. In 1961, as Muppets, Inc., grew, Jim and Jane brought on puppeteer and writer Jerry Juhl, and in 1963, after Jim and his family had moved to New York, master puppet builder Don Sahlin and puppeteer Frank Oz joined. Together, they helped develop the Muppets' first nationally known character, Rowlf the Dog, who appeared regularly on *The Jimmy Dean Show* from 1963 to 1966. Between 1964 and 1969, Jim produced several experimental films, including the award-winning *Time Piece*, *Youth '68*, and *The Cube*.

In 1966, a public television producer named Joan Ganz Cooney began work on a groundbreaking educational children's television show called *Sesame Street* that would premiere in 1969. Based on Jim's creative reputation, Cooney asked him to create a family of characters to populate *Sesame Street*. Jim also put his filmmaking skills to use in producing numerous counting films for the program.

Sesame Street demonstrated the Muppets' appeal to children, but Jim strongly believed these characters could entertain a much wider audience. After years of trying to sell the idea for *The Muppet Show* in the United States, Jim received backing from a London-based television producer, Lord Lew Grade. In 1975, production began at Grade's ATV Studios, and soon the world was introduced to this new family of characters. The success of *The Muppet Show* led to Hollywood, where the Muppets starred in six feature films, including *The Muppet Movie*, *The Great Muppet Caper*, and *The Muppets Take Manhattan*.

During the 1980s, in addition to making Muppet movies, Jim brought two remarkably original fantasy films to the big screen, *The Dark Crystal* and *Labyrinth*. Inspired by the artwork of British illustrator Brian Froud, these films challenged Jim to create new kinds of three-dimensional characters with advanced movement abilities. The multitalented staff that Jim gathered together to create these two films formed the basis for what is now known as Jim Henson's Creature Shop.

Throughout the 1980s, Jim also created memorable television series and specials. *Fraggle Rock* was one of the world's first international television coproductions. *Jim Henson's Muppet Babies*, an animated Saturday morning show, was awarded four consecutive Emmys for Outstanding Animated Program. *Jim Henson's The Storyteller* and *Jim Henson's The Storyteller: Greek Myths* were two original series conceived by Jim to convey the metaphoric richness of ancient stories. The result was a rare combination of ancient tradition and modern technological artistry.

Jim's last project was *Muppet*Vision 3-D*, a short multimedia film and interactive attraction, which he directed and which currently runs at custom-made theaters at Disney-MGM Studios theme park at the Walt Disney World Resort in Florida, and at Disney's California Adventure in Anaheim, California.

On May 16, 1990, after a brief illness, Jim Henson died in New York City, but his unique creative vision continues. Through the Jim Henson Company, Sesame Workshop, and, most recently, The Muppets Holding Company, his work continues to entertain a global audience.

Harry Belafonte, famed musician, actor, and human rights activist, appeared on *The Muppet Show* and *Sesame Street*. Both he and Jim were involved with UNICEF. (PAGE 163)

Candice Bergen appeared alongside the Muppets on *Saturday Night Live* and *The Muppet Show*. Jim also worked with her father, puppeteer Edgar Bergen, and shared a special relationship with their family. (PAGE 23)

Fran Brill has been a performer on *Sesame Street* since 1970. She has provided the show with many memorable characters, including Prairie Dawn and Zoe. (PAGE 90)

Bernie Brillstein, Jim's friend and agent since 1961, is the founding partner of Brillstein-Grey Entertainment. (PAGE 29)

Ray Charles, the much-beloved musician, appeared on *Sesame Street* and celebrated Jim's life on the television special *The Muppets Celebrate Jim Henson*. (PAGE 13)

Kevin Clash is best known for performing Elmo. He is the Muppet Captain for *Sesame Street*, and performs many other characters, including Hoots the Owl, Wolfgang the Seal, and Clifford, the emcee of *Muppets Tonight!* (PAGES 93 and 111)

Joan Ganz Cooney is cofounder of the Children's Television Workshop, now Sesame Workshop, the producers of *Sesame Street* since 1969. *Sesame Street* is seen in over 120 countries around the world. (PAGE 42)

John Denver, the popular singer/songwriter, was Jim's friend. He appeared on *The Muppet Show*, as well as the television specials *John Denver & The Muppets: A Christmas Together* and *John Denver & The Muppets: Rocky Mountain Holiday*. (PAGE 34)

Doc, played by Gerry Parkes in the show *Fraggle Rock*, is a human inventor who moves into a house with a hole in it that leads down to Fraggle Rock. (PAGE 167)

Dr. Teeth, with his gold tooth and glittering top hat, is the leader of the *Muppet Show* house band, Dr. Teeth & the Electric Mayhem. He was performed by Jim. (PAGES 53, 69, and 197)

Cotterpin Doozer is one of the hardworking race of Doozers who share *Fraggle Rock* with the Fraggles. (PAGE 56)

Bonnie Erickson worked with the Muppets starting in 1970 as a puppet builder and designer and was responsible for Miss Piggy, Statler and Waldorf, and others. (PAGE 94)

Ernie and **Bert** have been best friends and roommates on *Sesame Street* since 1969. Performed by Jim, Ernie always reveled in driving Frank Oz's Bert to distraction. (PAGES 24, 43, 88–89, 106–107, and 122–123)

Cantus Fraggle is a Minstrel who is keenly aware of the power of music, and a wise and loving teacher. He was specifically designed by the writers of *Fraggle Rock* for Jim to perform. (PAGES 17, 45, 47, 55, 67, and 129)

Gobo Fraggle is the brave and charming leader of the Fraggle

Five. He is an explorer, like his uncle, Traveling Matt Fraggle.
(PAGES 63 and 99)

Mokey Fraggle is an artist, poet, and philosopher, and is perhaps the most sensitive of the Fraggle Five. (PAGES 145 and 160)

Tony Geiss has been a writer, composer, and lyricist for *Sesame Street* and Children's Television Workshop since 1974, and a staff writer on *Sesame Street* since 1998. (PAGES 117 and 122–123)

Dave Goelz joined Jim as a designer in 1973, and became a performer of many characters, including the Great Gonzo and Professor Bunsen Honeydew in *The Muppet Show*, and Traveling Matt and Boober in *Fraggle Rock*. (PAGES 75, 96, and 130)

The Guitarist was a character in *The Cube*, a program Jim and Jerry Juhl wrote for NBC's Experiment in Television that aired in 1969. (PAGE 46)

Hal Hackaday and **Larry Grossman** have written many memorable songs. Larry Grossman was also a music consultant for *The Muppet Show*. (PAGE 31)

Brian Henson is Jim's older son, and is the co-CEO and cochairman of the Jim Henson Company. He is a puppeteer, producer, and director. His credits include *The Muppet Christmas*

Carol, *Muppet Treasure Island*, *Muppets Tonight!*, *Jack and the Beanstalk: The Real Story*, and *Farscape: The Peacekeeper Wars*. (PAGES 84 and 97)

Cheryl Henson is the second of Jim's five children. She is the president of the Jim Henson Foundation and a director of the Jim Henson Company. She executive produced the International Festival of Puppet Theater in New York from 1992 to 2000. She has been a puppet builder and is an author of the book *Muppets Make Puppets*. (PAGES 1–6)

Jane Henson, an artist and puppeteer, was Jim's first working partner, his wife, and is the mother of their five children. She founded the Jim Henson Legacy in 1993 and now serves on its board of directors. (PAGES 109 and 128)

Lisa Henson is Jim's eldest daughter and worked with him to develop the *Storyteller* series. She was president of Columbia Pictures from 1994 to 1996 and is now the co-CEO and cochairman of the Jim Henson Company. (PAGES 115, 142, and 158)

Jerry Juhl began working with Jim in 1961, first as a puppeteer and then as a writer for *Sesame Street*, *The Muppet Show*, and *Fraggle Rock*, as well as many other Muppet and non-Muppet projects, including the feature films *The Muppet Movie*, *The*

Great Muppet Caper, The Muppet Christmas Carol, Muppet Treasure Island, and *Muppets from Space*. (PAGES 18, 27, 38, 46, 57, 59, 60, 74, 148, and 152)

Kermit the Frog is the unflappable host of *The Muppet Show* and leader of the Muppet Gang. An early version of Kermit first appeared on *Sam and Friends*, and he is the only Muppet to regularly appear in both *Sesame Street* and Muppet productions. Jim performed Kermit from 1955 until his death. (PAGES 14–15, 20–21, 22, 59, 61, 65, 66, 74, 95, 114, 116, 126–127, 132, 140–141, 143, and 147)

David Lazer, executive producer of *The Muppet Show*, Vice Chairman Emeritus of The Jim Henson Company, and good friend, began working with Jim in 1965 as an executive at IBM. (PAGE 144)

Dennis Lee and **Philip Balsam** collaborated to write the songs for *Fraggle Rock* over the course of its four-year run, and wrote the music for the special *The Tale of the Bunny Picnic*. Dennis Lee is Toronto's first poet laureate. (PAGES 56, 63, 67, 85, 145, and 160)

Ma Otter is the kind and hardworking mother of Emmet Otter in the television special *Emmet Otter's Jug-Band Christmas*. (PAGES 131 and 155)

Anthony Minghella, the Academy Award–winning director of *The English Patient*, wrote all nine episodes of *Jim Henson's The Storyteller*. (PAGE 166)

Jeff Moss was a founding headwriter and composer-lyricist for *Sesame Street* and wrote Ernie's signature song, "Rubber Duckie." He also wrote the Academy Award–nominated music and lyrics for the songs in *The Muppets Take Manhattan*. (PAGES 53, 88–89, 106–107, 126–127)

Jerry Nelson began working with Jim as one of the core group of performers in 1965. His characters include the Count from *Sesame Street*, Floyd Pepper and Robin the Frog from *The Muppet Show*, and Gobo Fraggle from *Fraggle Rock*, among many others. (PAGE 33)

Frank Oz began working with Jim as a core performer in 1963. He is the man behind Fozzie Bear, Miss Piggy, and Animal on *The Muppet Show*, and Grover, Bert, and Cookie Monster on *Sesame Street*, among many others. An accomplished film director, his first directing credits were *The Muppets Take Manhattan* and as codirector with Jim on *The Dark Crystal*. (PAGES 35, 64, 81, 92, and 138)

Sam Pottle and **David Axlerod** were a composer and lyricist for

Sesame Street. Sam Pottle was the show's musical director after Joe Raposo and, with Jim, wrote the theme song for *The Muppet Show*. (PAGE 65)

Joe Raposo was an award-winning composer and lyricist with a diverse body of work, including Kermit's anthem, "Bein' Green." He was one of the creators of *Sesame Street* and was the show's first musical director. He also worked with Jim and the Muppets when he wrote the score for *The Frog Prince*, as well as the Academy Award–nominated score for *The Great Muppet Caper*. In addition to his work with the Muppets, he wrote music for Frank Sinatra, Ray Charles, Dr. Seuss, and others. (PAGES 14–15, and 24)

Robin the Frog, performed by Jerry Nelson, is Kermit's young but precocious nephew who first appeared in *The Frog Prince* in 1971 and appeared often in *The Muppet Show*. (PAGE 31)

Don Sahlin was a master puppet builder and designer. First hired by Jim in 1962 to build Rowlf the Dog, he went on to create a signature style for Muppet construction. (PAGE 98)

Donald Siegal was a composer and lyricist best known for his work for children's television, including *Sesame Street*. (PAGES 140–141)

Jocelyn Stevenson was a primary writer for *Fraggle Rock* and played an important role in developing the show. A close friend of Jim's, she was involved in numerous other Henson projects, including *Tale of the Bunny Picnic*, *The Ghost of Faffner Hall*, and *The Secret Life of Toys*. (PAGES 168–169)

Norman Stiles and **Christopher Cerf** are a former head writer of *Sesame Street* and a prolific composer and lyricist for the show. (PAGE 43)

Jon Stone was a producer, principal director, and head writer of *Sesame Street*. He worked closely with Jim in establishing the format, style, and many of the characters of the show. He and Jim worked together on numerous other projects starting in 1965. (PAGE 151)

The urSkeks from *The Dark Crystal* appear at the end of the film, as the healing of the Dark Crystal reunites the peaceful Mystics and the vile Skeksis into the form of the wise urSkeks, making for a dramatic finale to Jim's first fantasy project. (PAGE 157)

Steve Whitmire joined the Muppet family as a puppeteer on *The Muppet Show* in 1978, where he created the characters of Rizzo the Rat and others. In *Fraggle Rock* he performed Wembley and

Sprocket. Steve has performed Kermit the Frog and Ernie since Jim's death in 1990. (PAGE 79)

Paul Williams and **Kenny Ascher** wrote the Academy Award–nominated score for *The Muppet Movie*. Paul Williams also appeared on *The Muppet Show* and wrote the music and lyrics for *Emmet Otter's Jug-Band Christmas* and *The Muppet Christmas Carol*. (PAGES 20–21, 69, 95, 104, 131, 155, and 171)

Sources

All illustrations were drawn by Jim Henson, courtesy of
Henson Family Properties, LLC. Reprinted by permission of
Sesame Workshop, The Muppets Holding Co., LLC, and
The Jim Henson Company, Inc.

p. 123, Bert and Ernie are trademarks of Sesame Workshop
pp. 66, 86, 134, Kermit and "Muppet" are trademarks of
The Muppets Holding Co., LLC
All other illustrations and illustration on p. 86 © The Jim Henson
Company, Inc.

Jim Henson's words from letters, essays, lectures, and journals
© Henson Family Properties, LLC. Used by permission.
All Rights Reserved.

Materials courtesy of The Jim Henson Company, Inc.:

Fraggle Rock © 1982–1986 The Jim Henson Company, Inc. All Rights Reserved.

p. 56, "The Way I've Got to Go"; p. 47, "Face Facts : Pack Snacks : Make Tracks"; p. 67, "Ball of Fire"; p. 85, "Fraggle Rock Theme Song"; p. 145, "Show Me": Music and Lyrics by Phil Balsam and Dennis Lee

p. 160, "The Joy": Music and Lyrics by Phil Balsam and B. P. Nichol

p. 99, "Workin', Workin', Workin'" : Music and Lyrics by Don Gillis and Jerry Juhl

p. 17, "Mokey and the Minstrels"; pp. 47, 55, "The Minstrels"; p. 129, "The Honk of Honks": Scripts by Jocelyn Stevenson

p. 45, "The Bells of Fraggle Rock": Script by Jocelyn Stevenson (with Jerry Juhl and Susan Juhl)

p. 167, "The Trash Heap Doesn't Live Here Anymore": Script by Jerry Juhl

p. 46, *The Cube*: Script by Jim Henson and Jerry Juhl © 1969 The Jim Henson Company, Inc. All Rights Reserved.

p. 131, "When the River Meets the Sea"; p. 155, "Our World": Music and Lyrics by Paul Williams. *Emmet Otter's Jug-Band Christmas* © 1977 Hobbitron Enterprises/ASCAP. Used by Permission. All Rights Reserved.

p. 157, *The Dark Crystal*: Screenplay by David Odell © 1994, 1999 The Jim Henson Company, Inc. All Rights Reserved.
p. 23, "Yet Another Introduction" by Candice Bergen, *Jim Henson: The Works* by Christopher Finch, Jim Henson Company/Random House © 1993 Jim Henson Productions, Inc.
p. 97, "Introduction" by Brian Henson; 166, "Foreword" by Anthony Minghella: *No Strings Attached* by Matt Bacon, Macmillan © 1997 The Jim Henson Company, Inc. All Rights Reserved.

Materials courtesy of The Muppets Holding Co. © The Muppets Holding Co., LLC. All Rights Reserved.

pp. 20–21, "The Rainbow Connection"; p. 68, "Can You Picture That"; p. 95, "Movin' Right Along"; pp. 104, 171, "The Magic Store": Music and Lyrics by Paul Williams and Kenny Ascher. *The Muppet Movie*.
p. 59; p. 74: Screenplay by Jerry Juhl and Jack Burns. *The Muppet Movie*.
p. 53, "You Can't Take No for an Answer": Music and Lyrics by Jeff Moss. *The Muppets Take Manhattan*.
p. 60, Screenplay by Frank Oz, Tom Patchett, Jay Tarses. *The Muppets Take Manhattan*.
p. 143, "My Garden": *Kermit's Garden of Verses* by Jack Prelutsky, A Muppet Press Book. Random House Pub. (1982).

Other Material:

pp. 14–15, "Bein' Green": Music and Lyrics by Joe Raposo © 1970 Jonico Music, Inc.; © renewed 1998 by Green Fox Music, Inc. All Rights Reserved. Used by permission.
p. 24, "The Imagination Song": Music and Lyrics by Joe Raposo © 1972 by Muppet-Jonico Publishing Co.; © renewed 2000 by Green Fox Music, Inc. All Rights Reserved. Used by permission.

p. 31, "Just One Person": Music and Lyrics by Larry Grossman and Hal Hackaday. © Unichappell Music, Inc. All Rights Reserved. Used by permission. Warner Brothers Publications U.S. Inc., Miami, Florida 33014.

p. 34, "It's in Every One of Us": Music and Lyrics by David Pomeranz © 1973 (Renewed) WB Music Corp. and Upward Spiral Music. All Rights Administered by WB MUSIC CORP. All Rights Reserved. Used by permission. Warner Brothers Publications U.S. Inc., Miami, Florida 33014

pp. 88–89, "But I Like You" by Jeff Moss © 1983 by Festival Attractions, Inc. (ASCAP), Reprinted with permission. All Rights Reserved. International copyright secured.
pp. 106–107, "I Don't Want to Live on the Moon" by Jeff Moss © 1978 by Festival Attractions, Inc. (ASCAP), Reprinted with

permission. All Rights Reserved. International copyright secured. pp. 126–127, "Tadpole" by Jeff Moss © 1986 by Festival Attractions, inc. (ASCAP), Reprinted with permission. All Rights Reserved. International copyright secured.

p. 117, "Frogs in the Glen" by Tony Geiss is administered and licensed by Sesame Workshop. © 1982 Tony Geiss. Used by permission. All Rights Reserved.

pp. 140–141, "I Wonder 'Bout the World" by Donald Siegal is owned and licensed by Sesame Workshop. © 1990 Sesame Workshop. Used by permission. All Rights Reserved.

p. 41, "Wishing Song": Music and Lyrics by Paul Tracey. Copyright © 1974 Kunjani Music (ASCAP). All Rights Reserved. Used by permission.

p. 43, "Dance Myself to Sleep" by Christopher Cerf and Norman Stiles is owned and licensed by Sesame Workshop and Christopher Cerf d/b/a Splotched Animal Music. © 1981 Sesame Workshop and Christopher Cerf. Used by permission. All Rights Reserved.

p. 65, "This Frog" by Sam Pottle and David Axlerod is owned and licensed by Sesame Workshop. © 1977 Sesame Workshop. Used by permission. All Rights Reserved.

pp. 122–123, Script by Tony Geiss. *Sesame Street.*
Sesame Street excerpts provided courtesy of Sesame Workshop
(New York, NY). All Rights Reserved. Used by permission.

pp. 105, 112: *Homespun: Tales from America's Favorite
Storytellers* by Jimmy Neil Smith. Crown Publishers, October
1988.

pp. 25, 121: "The Muppets in Movieland." Article by John
Culhane, *New York Times Magazine*, June 10, 1979. © 1979,
John Culhane. Reprinted by permission.

Acknowledgments

We would like to thank the many contributors who let us use their quotes to create this book. Everyone has been so generous. We would also like to thank the many performers, writers, artists, friends, and family who we were not able to include here. Jim's life was rich with brilliant associates. He loved and relied on so many. We hope that we have conveyed the appreciation that he had for everyone who helped him to realize his many projects.

I would like to thank Karen Falk, the archivist for the Jim Henson Company, who was hired by my mother thirteen years ago to organize my father's papers. Although Karen never met my father, she knows what he left behind better than anyone. We could not have done this project without her. I also want to thank Nathaniel Wharton, who kept our manuscript organized and contributed many good ideas, and

Laurent Linn, whom I worked with on *Sesame Street* for eleven years and who was able to capture my father's humor in the design of this book so beautifully.

The many characters that Jim created are now owned by three different entities. We could not have done this book without all of their cooperation. In particular I would like to thank Chris Curtin and Debbie McClellan at The Muppets Holding Company, Gary Knell and Ellen Lewis at Sesame Workshop, and Peter Schube and Jamie Kershaw at the Jim Henson Company. We appreciate all of the people who keep the characters alive through new production. We also thank Joe Raposo's family, who let us use his song for our title.

Will Schwalbe, the editor in chief at Hyperion, was the second friend that I made when I went to college. He came to Jim's memorial service because he knew him as my father. Years later, he remembered the creative energy and warmth in what those who loved Jim had to say and suggested that we do this book. He put us together with our gracious editor, Mary Ellen O'Neill, who worked with us to make it happen. We are grateful to them for all of their insights and expertise.

I would like to thank my mother, Jane Henson, for reading each version of the manuscript as we collected and reorganized the many quotes, my brother John and my sister Heather, who are not quoted here but were no less a part of our dad's life, my husband, Ed Finn, who was my support, my baby, Declan, who squirmed on my lap through my one-handed typing, and my daughter, Elizabeth, who has loved Kermit since before she could walk.

And a special thank-you to everyone in the audience who found laughter and joy in watching the Muppets and all of Jim's work. It meant the world to him.

—*Cheryl Henson*

Message? I got no message! I'm a puppet, man. This is all sham...make believe! Like everything! Everybody! We're all puppets! That's why we gotta boogie boogie boogie!!!

—*Dr. Teeth*

THE JIM HENSON COMPANY

Celebrating 50 years of creativity,
technological achievement
and inspired silliness.
Visit www.henson.com

Join Kermit the Frog as he
celebrates 50 years of Being Green.
Visit www.muppets.com